Deep Inside My Mind

Abbey Hupp

BookLeaf Publishing

India | USA | UK

Presentation by *BookLeaf Publishing*

Web: www.bookleafpub.com

E-mail: info@bookleafpub.com

ISBN: 9789360946074

First edition 2024

Confessions

I confess my deepest sorrows
Before they completely consume me
Allowing them a glimpse of my soul
Trying to summon their response with watering
eyes and shaky hands
But the silence cuts me deep, leaving open
wounds on my chest
Dousing it with salt
My heart echoing in my chest, beating in my
ears, pulsing in my head
As the stillness fills me up like an itch a cannot
scratch like pain I cannot ease
I feel the knife sinking into my back
Their betrayal heavy on my skin pushing the
blade deeper and deeper

Pretty Pink Bow

I like to tie everything in a pretty pink bow
Especially my hair
My highlighted strands pulled back with a satin
ribbon
Sometimes I wish I could tie every thing in a
pretty pink bow
I could wrap up my feelings to make them more
appealing
Or I could use it to lace together the scars carved
deep into my heart
I wish I could put a bow on my trauma
Change the grey, wishy washy, terrors to a pink
arches of silk
But I cant, and until I can
I will just be the girl with the pretty pink bow in
her hair that wear her wounded heart on her
sleeve

When does childhood end?

When days on the playgrounds turn into days on
social media
And the child like freedom turns into bricks of
stress weighing on your back
Or when the innocent twinkle in your eyes glaze
over with the troubles and pain of adulthood

Superficial Mindset

After years of soul searching my mind is still
superficial
Stuck on the repeating thought 'how can I be
pretty'
Racking my brain on how to fix all my
imperfections
The pudge of my stomach that shows in all my
favorite skirts
Or the cellulite that ripples down the fat of my
legs
How about the stretch marks that run up my
body like roadmaps?
I would sign my life away to have my
insecurities lifted off my chest
So as my pointer and middle graze the back of
my throat
I don't feel even a bit guilty

Sometime I Daydream

Sometimes I daydream
Sometimes I daydream with my head slumped
against my hand as I attempt to escape my
crippling reality
Sometimes I day dream about my future
wedding or the boy from elementary school who
I never quite forgot
But sometimes I daydream about being
somebody else, actually, anyone else
Dreaming about what it would be like to be the
girl with the long silky hair and skin like
porcelain
About trading in my full cheeks and double chin
for the chiseled face of the girl who haunts my
thoughts
Sometimes I daydream about how fulfilling her
life must be
Perfect face, perfect body, perfect friends
Ignoring my life to dream about my ideal one
But the yearning fills me up
Scratching at my brain begging me to daydream
again

Decisions

How do you decide?
Between colleges and jobs
Doctor or actor?
How do you decide?
Which dreams are worth going after

Food for Fear

Food has always been a peaceful place
Indulging in cheesy pastas were the only thing to
bring me comfort
But, I grew up and became a teenage girl
Now, food is a fear
The heavy breads taunting the extra meat on my
bones
Counting the calories of everything I have to
consume
Comfort is suddenly a tricky thing
Because the only thing to provide me with
comfort is the empty feeling, that only skipping
out on meals brings me

Suck it up

Crybaby
That's what they call me
You wear your emotions on your face
That's what they tell me
Wow, someone's upset
That's what they whisper about me
Since when has feeling become a bad thing
Experiencing my deepest emotion isn't okay?
It's okay to not be okay
They pretend
Don't be afraid to cry
They write on billboards
Suck it up
That's what they really mean

hope

hope is dangerous
it gives women a false sense that they could ever
be safe
in a world like ours

Dirty, Disgusting, Used

Dirty
Disgusting
Used
Eight years old
Those words etching themselves into my head
Even after he peels his sweaty body off of mine
Those three words echoing in my thoughts
Keep this a secret he reminds me
Dirty
Disgusting
Used
Seven years have passed
And when I lie awake at night
I still feel his clammy hands all down my belly
and breasts
My own self hatred slicing open the scars he left
I will keep this a secret I promised him
Dirty
Disgusting
Used
Eight years old
Walking into my third grade classroom
A piece of himself still aching between my legs
The world seeming to spin slower that day

His filthy touch burning a hole directly through
my flesh and leaving his mark on my soul
You're a good girl he whispers
Dirty
Disgusting
Used
Seven years have passed
Although the to the skin my wounds have healed
over, his cuts run much deeper
Looking in the mirror has become a burdened
task
His hand prints still shadowed over my most
intimate spaces
No matter the scrubbing I do or the tears I let fall
he will always be all over me
On my chest, my neck, and my thighs
A piece of me will always belong to him
I don't want to be your good girl I wish I
whispered back
Dirty
Disgusting
Used

What's so bad about a compliment?

come on baby show me a smile
13 years old
that was the first time my soul was dampened
with a dirty stare
great tits
still 13 years old
my insides twisted as the the words add to the
branding on the depths of who i am
how much for a night?
14 years old
i think his wink made it worse
please show me your body
only a few weeks older
i think my innocence is chipping away a little bit
more as i reread the sentence on my screen
you're nothing but a body
15 years old
is this all i am? a brainless body to be perceived
by men too many years older than me
are you pure?
15 years still
i don't feel like it anymore i've had enough dirty
attention to have my innocence crumbled to dust
what's so bad about a compliment?

too young for this
the intention behind your words tells me they are
anything but a compliment

Hands meet Skin

Hands all over my skin
Scared
Worried
Agony
Hurt
Scared
Damaged
Pained
Overwhelmed
Scared
My skin, with hands all over it
Love
Lust
Bashful
Comfort
Love
Safe
Warmth
Delight
Love
Hands crushing skin
Violence
Blood
Pain
Abuse

Violence
Cruel
Brutal
Destruction
Violence
Hands meet skin

Loveable

my whole life i've wanted and begged God for a
boyfriend
someone to hold my hand
to play with my hair
or leave little notes in my locker
i begged and yearned for someone to accompany
me when my best friends went on first dates or
whispered with their crushes in the halls
but now i yearn and wonder if i really want a
boyfriend or if i just want to prove i am loveable
after all

Flowers

17

The delicate petals and strong stems that add
vibrant colour to our dull, heartless world
Waiting to be ruined by the human hand

Daisy

18

Silky white, plush yellow centers, fragile leaves
Blooming from the dirt
In the full green meadows
No voice, no lungs, no breath

I Hate School

I hate school
Mean girls lurking behind lockers
School work adding weight to my shoulders
Embarrassment seeping through every one of
my actions
But what makes me hate school most of is fear
The news flooded with stories of kids my age
being shot in their homerooms
Their brains being splattered from the office to
the courtyard
Bodies piling up in corridors
The hatred I hold for the building that gathers
children to wait for their lives to end before they
can really begin
How can anyone not hate school?

will you still love me?

will you still love me?
when my skin is dry
and my body aches
will you still want me?
when i shut my mind down
and keep to myself
will you still need me?
when all i do is cry
and the clouds behind my eyes are only grey and
stormy
will you still love me?

anybody else

I think i've finally come to terms
with what's running through my veins is the
blood of a girl i can't stand
and pumping through my heart is the want to be
anybody else